Fat Poets Speak 3

FatDance Flying

Frannie Zellman, Editor

Fat Poets' Society
Kathy Barron, Durette Hauser,
Lesleigh Owen, Frannie Zellman

New Voices
Tolonda Henderson, Dawn Howard,
Miranda Jacobson, Kris Owen,
Michelle Kriz Parkinson,
Sherrie Myers

AF473537

Pearlsong Press
Nashville, TN

Pearlsong Press
P.O. Box 58065 | Nashville, TN 37205
www.pearlsong.com | www.pearlsongpress.com

© 2020 Frannie Zellman

Trade paperback ISBN: 9781597190954
Ebook ISBN: 9781597190961
Book & cover design by Zelda Pudding

Also by Frannie Zellman:

Fat Poets Speak: Voices of the Fat Poets' Society (Ed.)
Fat Poets Speak 2: Living and Loving Fatly (Ed.)
FatLand: A Novel | *FatLand: The Early Days*

No part of this book may be reproduced, stored in or introduced into a retrieval system, or transmitted, in any form or by any means (electronic, mechanical, photocopying, recording, or otherwise), without the written permission of the publisher, with the except of brief quotations included in reviews.

Library of Congress Cataloging-in-Publication Data

Names: Zellman, Frannie, 1954–editor.
Title: Fat poets speak 3 : fatdance flying / Frannie Zellman, editor.
Description: Nashville, TN : Pearlsong Press, [2020] | Series: Fat poets speak ; 3 | Fat Poets' Society: Kathy Barron, Durette Hauser, Lesleigh Owen, Frannie Zellman; New Voices: Tolonda Henderson, Dawn Howard, Miranda Jacobson, Kris Owen, Michelle Kriz Parkinson, Sherrie Myers,. |
Summary: "The Fat Poets' Society writes about their joys, sorrows, anger, sadness, and pleasure at living in a world that constantly tries to reject and inhibit fat people. Volume 3 of the Fat Poets Speak series, Fat Poets Speak 3: FatDance Flying, comprises poems in which the poets alternately dance and fly, moving their feet and their bodies and then growing wings as they encompass the earth, above the earth, and finally, the sky, breaking the bodily barrier. To all who choose to read this volume, they say, "Come dance and fly with us.""—Provided by publisher.
Identifiers: LCCN 2020022915 (print) | LCCN 2020022916 (ebook) | ISBN 9781597190954 (trade paperback) | ISBN 9781597190961 (ebook)
Subjects: LCSH: American poetry—Women authors. | Overweight persons—Poetry.
Classification: LCC PS589 .F384 2020 (print) | LCC PS589 (ebook) | DDC 811/.60803561—dc23
LC record available at https://lccn.loc.gov/2020022915
LC ebook record available at https://lccn.loc.gov/2020022916

Dedicated to the members of
the Fat Lip Readers Theatre (1981-1999),
who brought the world laughter
with fattitude.

CONTENTS

Introduction

It is 2020, and "fat shaming" is now a thing, featured in articles, blogs, podcasts, and social media throughout not only the USA, but other nations as well. People of size—yes, fat people—have won Grammys—-thinking of Lizzo here!—and homecoming queen contests. Clothing for fat people is available in more places online and in-store than ever before. Health At Every Size® (HAES®) appears in more, and more prominently in, citations for articles and journals than at any time in its proud history.

And yet—

Most doctors still tell fat patients to lose weight, regardless of our conditions or problems, and regardless of the fact that restricting ourselves into smaller bodies cures nothing and may even cause serious harm. The diet of the month still features prominently in magazines we pass near the check-out lanes of supermarkets. "The Biggest Loser," the television show mercifully terminated a few years back, is being resurrected.

In spite of the reappearance of this toxic filth—or perhaps partly because of its horrifying lessons—the word will continue to spread across the land and the world: Fat people don't need fixing! Attitudes about them do. But not fast enough or far enough.

Strange how at times we are still way too visible to people determined to hate us, and yet invisible. The language of the Fat Positivity and Fat Acceptance movements is now coopted by weight loss companies and franchises: "wellness" instead of "diet." It is increasingly clear to many people that "diet" equals "weight cycling" and a gateway to disordered eating and actual illness. And yet, like those who saw that the Emperor had no clothes, they cannot bring themselves to state the obvious.

So what do we say, what do we do?

We write. We dance. We are. We fly.

At a workshop for NAAFA (the National Association to Advance Fat Acceptance), Lesleigh Owen, one of the poets featured in this book, asked participants to talk about movement, how it felt to move in their bodies, and how they would express these thoughts in writing. It is from this workshop that the idea for Volume 3 of the *Fat Poets Speak* series was born.

Somehow a vital piece of being a fat person at home or at least content in their skin includes moving and dancing and flying. Ragen Chastain is another inspiration for this book as she dances her own way to fat pride.

And yet many of us dance and fly in different ways, as well—in our minds, in our chairs, in our feelings. We move as we talk, as we imagine. And often we imagine how life might be if we lived without stigma.

The more of us who imagine fat liberation and who write about it, and who live it, the closer it comes.

Fat Lilith

"The Days of Fat Lilith" comprises the second part of this book.

Lilith, as some of you know, was originally a wind spirit of Sumerian origin. She is cited in the Talmud as the first wife of Adam, the one who refused to walk behind him. The legend she inspired was also that of a seductress who brought sexual dreams to men at night. And yet, as with many female forces and deities, she carries a significance of being, of living in several dimensions in fullness and complexity.

I see her as possessing the ability to be any size she wishes, to span the sky, to dance, to float, and to enjoy her force and, yes, life force. I see her as being amused by and lovingly sorry for the humans among whom she touches down at times.

I follow a timeline that creates her as the daughter of Inanna, also Sumerian, the goddess of love, creation, and, yes, war. Similarly I write her as the mother of Astarte, the Canaanite/Semitic goddess of love.

And I also see her as having lessons to impart: lessons of freedom of movement, of experiencing ease in one's body whatever its size, of flying and love of living.

Goddesses can and should be fat whenever they wish!

I hope you, our readers, will fatdance and fly with us through our days, whether from your living room, your stage, your seat, or your mind.

On behalf of the poets of *Fat Poets Speak 3: FatDance Flying,*

Frannie Zellman
Editor and contributor

PART I

THE FATDANCE

Lesleigh Owen

Monster World

Imagine a world
in which we worship monsters,
a world turned upside down,
where conformity and sameness
horrify us,
cause us to shield our children's eyes
and shriek in delicious horror,
all the while knowing
we're safe in our difference,
monsters with an endless supply
of heroes to kidnap
and skyscrapers to climb.

A world where scars are holy,
neurodiversity heralded,
where priests compose hymns to pendulous,
jiggling bellies.
A world in which aliens colonize
and scarecrows
bring comfort.

I would be a high priestess:
Pre-coffee crankiness celebrated,
crow's feet adored,
buck teeth revered.
Devotees would slouch downward,
dangling like my heavy breasts.
Nuns and monks would devote their lives
to interpreting my scrawl of stretch marks,

deciphering my bodily braille.
Acolytes would pen poems
praising the puffiness of my sacred cankles.

Monsters would crush and growl,
sacrificing girdles, IQ tests, and steep curbs
to our blistering wrath
while the masses shrieked and danced,
wrinkles flashing,
wheelchairs sparking,
hands signing,
upper arms clapping,
and crooked teeth
always grinning.

Kathy Barron

Goddess Incarnate

My body
is my temple.
I worship
my own pleasure.
My sensuality,
my guiding light.
Rolls of sensual flesh,
open receptors
of inspiration,
of delight,
of connection.

Hefty, solid, weighty,
light, graceful, warm.
A hymn book
of songs to sing
with love.

Dawn Howard

Squirrel

Fat black squirrel
sitting in my tree,
begging for a nut or seed
as he chatters at me.

His tail is all fluffed up
in his adorable display of attitude,
as if he's thinking "Why is the human laughing?
Hmmmph! Humans are so rude!"

I reach toward him with a shelled peanut.
He looks at me suspiciously,
his little head cocked to one side.

I ask him to come to me.
I want to see his beautiful black fur.
Come to me, roly poly friend.
I've only seen the likes of you in Michigan.
My pudgy little friend steps closer.
His tiny paw reaches out.
He grabs the peanut and scurries away.
All I see is his round little butt.

Michelle Kriz Parkinson

Dear Little One

You are always going to be fat.
Now stop crying and listen to me.

You are always going to be fat,
and sometimes the world
will be unkind to you
because of it.
Be kind to yourself instead.

You are always going to be fat,
and sometimes you
will encounter barriers
because of it.
Smash them to pieces.

You are always going to be fat,
and sometimes people who love you
will hurt you
because of it.
Love them even harder.

You are always going to be fat,
and sometimes you
will feel inferior
because of it.
Trust in your own greatness always.

You are always going to be fat,
and sometimes people

will tell you you're all wrong
because of it.
And sweet child, hear me
when I tell you
they're all wrong.

You are always going to be fat,
and sometimes you
will want to change yourself
because of it.
Sweet child, hear me
when I tell you
there's no need.

Lesleigh Owen

1981

We lived on the poor side of town;
me, my mom,
and two older sisters,
whose much smaller hand-me-downs
passed me by on the way to
thinner cousins.
I wore thrift-store purple faux-fur coats
and red-checkered pants
whose polyester stretched and scratched
before hipsters could
label me cool.

I trudged each day to school
and back.
For dinner, and from
Mother Hubbard cupboards,
we ate cereal with watered-down milk.
Christmas found us feasting
from greasy cardboard boxes
mass produced by the church.
I fingered my mother's paystubs
and marveled at four whole dollars per hour.

Too young to know better,
I stepped on the scale
at the pay-as-you-can doctor's clinic.
"Too fat," the doctor clucked.
Solemnly, she presented me with
the sacred book:

How to Lose Weight the Fun Way!
I could eat whole cups of
unsalted, unbuttered popcorn
and endless cans of sugar-free pop!
The cartoon pictures featured round,
smiling children with White faces
who found joy in overflowing bowls
of plain iceberg lettuce.

I returned home
to empty cupboards
to ponder how to eat less
and further water down the milk.

Lesleigh Owen

Love Letter

Dear Lesleigh:

It has come to my attention that you are—
how do I delicately state this?—
large, rotund, corpulent,
fatter than a tub of
sopping movie theater popcorn—
like how the popcorn drips,
you know, coating your fingers
with salty gold
that remains lickable for hours—
uh, fat. You know. Really fat.

I am concerned. With a capital C.
Just think of all those rolls, those crevices,
filled as I imagine they are with
happy dinners, the sweet tang
of orange cinnamon rolls,
and memories of your fat,
independent grandmother
who rode horses, dyed her hair bright red,
and painted pictures of freedom.

Oh, won't you think of your health?
Those numbers that suck the fat and character
from your grandness
till nothing but small,
black numbers remain.

And those movements!
Rippling through space,
jiggling like laughter and
smoky grape jelly
while businesspeople shroud themselves
in pantyhose and ties.
Movements that turn
space into a dance floor,
air into music.

But, but—I am horrified!
Truly, profoundly,
unequivocally dismayed.
Your belly, heavy and unforgettable,
claps its laughing pleasure.
Your chin supports your father's dimple
and waves of wondrous words.
Your arms wave in 2/2 time.
A symphony of senses
to which my body sways.

Outraged. I am outraged!
Your body crushes the scale,
dwarfs prefabricated silhouettes,
swims in brightness and sound.
I shiver in your broad shadow,
trembling at your fat, flat feet.
I look up, and up,
into mounds of whipped cream flesh

and compassionate eyes.

I am—
There are—
You should—
I beg you, madam,
remember my words,
my concern,
my righteous horror
and selfless shame.
My eternal contemplation
of your greatness.

I remain,
forever,
your humble servant.

Durette Hauser

Store

Panic sets in.
The food I choose
should be nobody's choice.
What tastes good
and is healthy for me,
my business.
I rarely go to a grocery store,
as the fear of judgment is always there.
Feeling hot and shaking by the time I meet the cashier.
Nearly crying as people look upon the contents of my
cart.
Yes, I enjoy ice cream and cake.
Don't you?
I also enjoy brussels sprouts and green beans.
But you see the ice cream and my anxiety peaks, feeling
a sadness.
Foods I love also nourish me.
Your judgment doesn't, so turn away, fool.

Miranda Jacobson

Fat

the first time
I don't remember exactly
imagining
double chinned baby
a healthy baby
a fat baby

remembrance is
you don't want to be fat
being rail thin
approaching teenage years
thinking of being fat
fat fat fat
family on a diet
entire family
I MUST BE fat
was rail thin

teased by my grandfather
"looks like you are getting fat"
mortified

am I looking fat
because
my family is on a diet?

fat fat fat

Kris Owen

The Dance

Sweet melodies of chocolate and coffee,
famished, I draw her close.
Her chest against mine, I pull her in.
We sway.
Her hips gently glide while her feet perform miraculous
feats.
Awe.
Dancing upon the boundaries of society,
dipping across barriers.
Seduced by scents of Love.
Separation. Subsumption.
The final act is always a Solo.

Michelle Kriz Parkinson

A Tune

There are notes that cause
my hips to shift
my shoulder to raise
my head to turn
my toes to lift
immediately, involuntarily nearly
imperceptibly.

They find me lost
in fog or project or traffic
and with the tiniest flick,
pull and twist
and curl
my lip

and when the strings tangle and bind
I hunt.
All precision and purpose
and planned abandon.
They cannot find me unaware
if I seek them,
arms reaching hips
swaying
hair tangling with
the curl
of my lip.

Lesleigh Owen

Physics of Dance

I dance a right hefty jig,
arms stretched out,
wings slapping a
syncopated rhythm
of freedom and sex.
Snapping, whirling,
bending far too low
for cracklin' old knees.
Dusty notes booming
like cracks of thunder
between my thighs.

My belly, a dangling timepiece,
bounces old beats.
boom, ba-boom, bam.

Partner?
Oh, girl, who needs one of them?
Somebody who rattles
like a single piece of paper?
Somebody smaller,
less acquainted with gravity?
Somebody whose movements
creak along a single plane,
slapped a-tween two dimensions
while my hip thrusts
shake the heavens?

And besides,

doesn't this body take
enough space for two?
(Or three, if you're willing
to cram.)
My head movements alone
demand their own dance floor.

Gunshot beats
pound bones into
chalk, useful for teaching
you all the laws of physics.
Oh,
it's dance time, sweet things:
Time to munch the dance floor
like supermarket cake,
time to slap audacious minutes
into sweaty hours,
time to remind the earth
how to spin.

Lesleigh Owen

Halloween

Halloween,
when jack-o-lanterns
grin at their roundness
and plump disks of sugar shiver
in plastic dresses.
When darkness, like patches
between a fat woman's thighs,
sighs and spreads
and children screech and claw—
this time in solidarity.

I am Halloween,
whispered secrets grown louder
as the light fades,
shimmering eyes
beneath costumes designed
to scare the devil from
our doorsteps,
an 18-ton, lumbering monster
neutered by giggles and
gingerbread houses.

I am Halloween,
round like doorknobs,
like fanged mouths
painted greasy red and
pursed to
demand recognition
and succor.

Kris Owen

Nosferatu

Cream triangles clicking into place.
Their tightness, noticeable against my mouth.
Sharp. Pointed. Fierce. Ready.
Beauty and beast.
Terror within my mouth.
Paleness I smooth across my cheeks,
lessening my life that throbs inside.
Darkness under my green depths,
and hallowing of my candy-appled cheeks.
Death.
Blood. Red. Roses.
Shrouding in shadows.
Cape flowing as I bend air, slicing it with my presence.
I am infinite.
Immortal.

Frannie Zellman

Fat Dance

Skin sweat
gold dust
in every crevice
every shake
every fold
She loves the men
who pleasure her body

with their eyes.

Frannie Zellman

Fat

How old was I? Six?
The doctor mouthed
the word as if
it were a life sentence,
a gunshot
hitting my soft
child's belly.

How strange,
to curse
round
and make it
dirty.

Doctor, the prison
was all your own.

Frannie Zellman

To Frannie, from Ricardo

You have chosen
to style yourself
Frannie,
and I don't mind
knowing you by
several different names,
as long as they encompass
and play to your sense
of the fine, the ridiculous,
the acute, the blissful.
I know you don't usually
discuss your bodily attributes,
but I always thought
your body was beautiful,
even when I tried to hide
my love of fat women
when I was channeling
white blond slim.
I remember when you gave
me long, oily massages
and I wanted to give you
one, too.
So from beyond dimensions,
beyond several spans of time,
beyond places we visited
and didn't visit,
I say to you, I wanted you

in a way that even you
cannot imagine.
I wanted your springing
perkily impudent breasts
and I wanted your carefully
deprecatory yet perennially
amused soul
and I wanted your long soft
legs to entwine with mine
every Sunday
from the living room
of your grandparents' apartment
even though they might have
been shocked,
although they were pretty cool
in their way
and might have understood
that the half-Jewish half-Puerto Rican boy
from the Bronx
was loving their granddaughter up in
her luscious fat self

and ombre, winking, entrancing soul.

Frannie Zellman

Muffin

I am fat Muffin.

I am orange striped
and basically quite philosophical,
except for when it comes to
fish, during the eating
of which I will sing a roisterers'
chorus in the key of G,
although my human tells me
that I go flat at times. I then ask
how a fat cat could go flat,
but I don't think he understands me.
Men!

However, I must say
that he makes the condo
fairly comfortable for me
and has furnished
an excellent window seat
with cushions from which
I look out at buildings, traffic
and birdies. I bear no malice
toward birdies
and would befriend them
if they wished,
But for some reason
they seem to find my presence
less than happymaking
even though I sing birdsongs to them

or what my human describes
as cat in the key of bird.
He is a musician, in case
you haven't guessed.
He rubs some strange looking box
with strings he keeps telling me
were not made of my friends' guts,
although I know better.
Still, I regard his occupation
as mostly harmless
and am inclined to be petted
when he has finished the weird rubbing.

His name is Michael.
I wanted to be named Muffin,
but he calls me Nadia.

Go figure.

Frannie Zellman

Fativusites

Why did they make
Cupid a sexless boy?
Make him a fat, husky,
sexed man
beloved of both men and women
along with his sister, Cupida,
a fat, proud lusty dame.
She should really be the one
to shoot the arrows.

And make the wine
sing and dance under full moons.
No need to tear people apart.
They can just howl a bit,
retreat to tents
and sleep
after fruiting
sweet
dripping chins.
Full round bellies.

No need for guilt.
Or shame.
Fativusites.
They're coming.

Part II

Flying

Tolonda Henderson

Fly

I used to have these callouses on my hands
and I miss them. Flying trapeze class
was the first physical activity I pursued
because of how good it made me feel
rather than how thin it might make my body,
and running my fingers along the rough
sore skin reminded me that it was only
a matter of time before I could get back
to the tent. It didn't matter that my body type
had been all wrong for dance or that I
was the largest student at the school.
As long as I worked with someone
of appropriate height and strength
I could flip myself upside down, hang
by my pudgy knees, and hold my body
still as it rose above the net such that someone
could reach out and pluck me from the air.

Refilling my class card became my top
priority: everything else was calculated
accordingly. I could eat lunch at Chipotle
every day in a week, or I could take a flying
trapeze class. Go to an Indigo Girls concert
or take a flying trapeze class. Buy a new set
of Harry Potter novels just because
they have new covers, or take three
flying trapeze classes.

Then the manager told me the school had instituted
a weight limit. He thought it might serve as motivation,
but I threw out my scale years ago, so what I heard
him say was reject the tyranny of the Body Mass Index
or take a flying trapeze class. Keep the insanity
of the diet industry at bay, or take a flying trapeze
class. Live fabulously in the body I had, or take
one more flying trapeze class.

I asked for a refund on my class card
because even if I were to become smaller
it would not be me who got to fly.

Kris Owen

Flying

I brush you with my arms as I walk inside you,
canned air infiltrating my lungs.
Your sardined insides afloat with masses who breathe
 a sigh of relief when I walk past.
I strut to my assigned number and pop myself into
 your shrinking seat.
Panic.
Is your safety measure going to fit this time?
Yes.
Will it the next time?
Perhaps.
For now, I wait in anticipation, and give me the damn
 Biscoff cookie.

Michelle Kriz Parkinson

Space

"You need to be aware
of all the space
you take up,"
she sneered, her eyes glancing
to her friends for giggles
and to me for disgust.

It was a look practiced
to magnify and shrink
in the same flash,
as if she were some kind
of magician.

"Sorry," I spit,
apologizing on behalf
of my overloaded backpack
for daring to disrupt
the papers on her desk.

So small and so giant.
Diminished and enlarged.
And in that apology,
the rage of a thousand aisles and armrests.
YOU need to be aware of all the space I take up;
it is no more or no less than I deserve.
You cannot claim what is rightfully mine
and I will not shrink myself
to fit your narrow vision.

Michelle Kriz Parkinson

Invocation

Dear Adiposia,
I pray to you:
Show me every imaginable shape
and stretch my vision to picture more.
Satisfy my every question
and fill me with unquenchable curiosity.
Allow me to taste but not hunger
and drink but not thirst.
Surround me with love that's never too much
and always enough.
Amen, amen, amen, amen.

Michelle Kriz Parkinson

Manatee

Content to float
unbothered,
my skin is thick,
but not so impenetrable
it can't be scarred.

I've made no enemies
for myself and yet
I am the enemy
of convenience
and speed and sport.

I sing to you of times long ago
when I could lure you to
the water
and your sleep
would become
my rest.

Michelle Kriz Parkinson

Getaway

We reach the shoreline
and exhale—
the furniture, the bodies,
the laughter here
are all sturdy and strong.

We remember how to frolic,
moment by moment,
as seascape
crashes into landscape
and erodes doubt.

We drip with saltwater
and the juice
of candy-sweet fruits—
even they refuse
to be delicate.

We sleep, wrapped
in the memory
of our weightlessness,
sunlight piercing our eyelids
and coloring our dreams.

Miranda Jacobson

Video Rental

"Some candy with that rental?"
"No thanks,
trying to watch my sugar intake."
"Betcha could eat a pizza in one sitting,"
laughing.

Betcha get minimum wage at this career path job.
Betcha only part-time pay.
Betcha no benefits as a side with that part-time pay.
Betcha still living in your parents' basement
playing video games.
Betcha people call you loser,
or don't even—
they put that thumb and forefinger salute
on their heads.
Betcha no synapses firing in that pea brain.
How many languages do you speak?

When was the last time YOU ate?
Make sure those winds buzzing
through our state
don't blow you down
in one fell sweep.

Out to get a pepperoni pizza,
extra cheese, to go
with this video,
and yeah, maybe I'll have a few pieces.

Miranda Jacobson

Childlike Satisfaction

burdensome yoke
worry

creates fear
reality

outward control freaks
inward control freaks

remain calm
quiet

life
enjoy
food
enjoy
sunshine
enjoy

surround yourself

self worth
arms of self worth
self
others

you are you
not false
fake

not
photoshopped

remember
re-member yourself

a child
reborn
free
be
your
self

Durette Hauser

Tia Sleeps

Tia sleeps
on her mommy at night
warm soft belly to belly
cozy like chocolate
smoky black eyes
gazing
warm grey coat of fur
rubs fat love
sweet life

Durette Hauser

Nipply

tingling
nipple to nipple

fat girl to fat girl

hug
big fat girl hug

Frannie Zellman

Cocoon

The small grass
near the rail
held that orange lacy
plant, supposedly
a weed.
In the autumn,
old cocoons.
A few purple flowers.
As we walked,
you stopped
and took my finger.
Rubbing it on the cocoon
that had been.
You said, "Frannie,
isn't it soft?"
Your eyes
ranged over
my chest, then lower
to my gently rounded
stomach,
lazing deliberately
over the soft foam
of one thigh,
then the other.
The sun hit
each of our mouths,
warming what
we might have said
as if it were a body

waiting to leave
the poor skin
and fly.

Abruptly you
dropped my fingers,
letting the slow,
censorious world in
once more.
"Come on,"
you said,
now ashamed of
loving the fat girl.
"Let's go back."

The rest of the day
I didn't know whether
to cry or grin.

At some point
in another season
a butterfly
would take wing.
A new cocoon
would form.
But not in the same
spot.
I knew
that I could never

hate you.

How I hated loving
you.

Frannie Zellman

Forest Park

The grass and I
are friends.
I press my back
to it
and don't even
worry insects.
I can tell
it's a dream
and yet
I've been there
so often
I could recite
the names
of flowers
I don't trample.
They're off to one side.
I am soft all over
and lift pear breasts
until they're in
a trance.

Have I traced
clouds
or fought,
like Don Quixote,
to move air?

Lesleigh Owen

Flesh Talk

Stop.
Open your eyes.
Close your mouth.
Think quiet thoughts
or none at all.
Listen.
Sounds whisper, sigh,
drone in a monotone
too easy to ignore,
crouching as they do
behind the creak
of spoken words.
The snarl of empty bellies,
groan of interrupted opinions,
whistle of asthmatic breaths,
clack of teeth on
some kind of bone,
a wheeze like a wet cough
as flesh remembers to let go,
to open to voices, tongues,
and ears finally
ready to hear.
There exists a time,
just after midnight,
when moonlight paints
dark skin darker
and bellies clap beats
on chapped red thighs.
If you stop talking—

just one quiet, unplugged minute—
you can just hear the
snap and gasp of thoughts
birthed in skin.

Lesleigh Owen

Fatphobe

Fatphobe, I'm onto you.
Your eyes that linger,
the roll and drip of your tongue over words,
sharp and pointed,
fashioned to penetrate and invade.
Your lips that curl upward,
millimeter away from a kiss
and a sigh,
echoing in negative the
salty droop of rolls toward
gravity's breathless grasp.

Loop around my body,
caressing with hoops, swirls—
and the occasionally misspelled word—
never quite knowing,
masticating
doughy, kneadable mounds
that spread outward like a banquet.

Fatphobe, I'm onto you.
If you stop hating me,
will I still be here?
Or will I melt back into the
soft, rhythmic world
where dancing jiggles happy bodies,
definitions brunch beneath fat feet,
and scales belong only on fish?

Fatphobe, I'm onto you:
Angry, spitting, furious,
tap-tap-homicidal-only-because-I'm-concerned-tap,
eat a salad, fattie,
crush your body
into something smaller and transparent,
like Cinderella's glass slipper.
So mad, hate you,
hope your heart attack kills you tomorrow
because you don't hate you enough
and I've always been a helper.

Fatphobe, I'm onto you.
You creep around,
beside, above, between,
but never within.
I exist in complete roundness,
unapologetic,
impenetrable of mandated looks.

Kris Owen

Fatphobe

Scarlet against ivory,
I await "The Choice."
Seconds drag their nails across the open face.
Judgment comes just before sitting.
Tip-tap against your phone.
Studying everything else before you,
except the neglected space before you:
me.
A feigned smile,
polite.
Glossed.
Professional.
It doesn't hide the horrified scream behind your eyes.
I am your monstrosity.
You want me to return to my West Wing,
a Beast for all time.
I will not apologize for my greatness.
I do not apologize for making your demons play.
Run from me.
I am too powerful for you.
You cannot satisfy me.
Run from me and hate yourself in the darkness.
I will not be your light.
I will not sustain you with my Love.
Your choice has consequences,
Coward.

Part III

No-Diet Day Poems

Frannie Zellman

The Box

Dieting is like
trying to sit
in the wrong box.
Cat sits, feet first,
but then realizes
that his body
still hangs,
soft and furry,
belly luminescent,
in tiers of round
protest
at having tried
to fit
in the box
his humans never
intended for him.

Or did they?

Frannie Zellman

Gaslighting

This, this
is our real hunger game—
trying to subsist
and smile
on calories
we feel we've
stolen
from the
overweening temptations
of fridge, closet,
pantry
and the smiles
of the Before and After
photos in the magazines.

What they don't tell you
is that eating feels a lot better
than starving

and that there is
an "after" the "after"
when your body
tells you enough
and takes back
all the nights
you went without
and returns them
with interest.

"Before" was happier
before the unhappiness
that was supposed
to render
you happy.

Frannie Zellman

Better Than Love

Not in one moment,
but in waves.
The way you know
you're going to leave
a lover
who no longer loves
but you're too inert
with broken promises
to confront the thing.

So you go on,
well, not go on,
but push to one side,
played out, loved away,
fireless,
until the calls cease.

But when you stop dieting
it's better than love
because your soul
looks not in the mirror
but in the cabinet
and finds something
much tastier
than regret.

Sherrie Myers

Hungry

I was playing bingo
and eating a hot dog.
The girl across from me
paid no heed
to her cards
but watched me
with an avidity
and a focus
that made me nervous.
Then I realized that she was dieting
and had no room
in her life
for anything
but hunger.

Sherrie Myers

We Abjure

We abjure
life and celebration

We offer up
our hopes
our dreams
our accomplishments
and our needs

sacrificing
on the altar
of the social norm

as we wait
a salvation
that never comes.

Sherrie Myers

The Instant I Stopped Dieting

I had been at it
three months.

Every day
every thought
centered:
what
could I eat
when
could I eat
how much
could I eat.

I was ravenous.

That day
when dinner
arrived at last

I ate slowly
trying
to stretch
toward the impossibility
of satiation.

Each bite
a struggle
not to
lose control
not to consume
the meagerness
too soon.

A single pea,
green and beautiful,
escaped my plate
rolling in slow motion
onto the floor.

I pursued it
under the table,
crawling.

Seizing my prize
I popped it into my mouth,
tasting victory.

As I sat on the floor
under my kitchen table
I realized
what I had done
and I understood.

There
was no victory
here,
only madness.

And I was free.

Sherrie Myers

I Pity

I pity
the poor dudes
on Madison Avenue
now that we
no longer need them
to decree
what constitutes
happiness.

Frannie Zellman

My Yard

My yard
greets me
in the same place
as the deer passed
two weeks ago.
I do not garden,
but the grass
near my body
waves, miles better
than clothes.

I emerge,
green-bound,
breasts almost
but not quite touching
the strands.

I was hoping to shock
the neighbors
by jiggling,
but they keep inside

robbed of the glories
of my swinging belly

and a world
in which we
could all sun dance.

Sherrie Myers

Skyclad

I recline in my garden,
skyclad.

A sybarite
reveling

in the summer breeze
skimming
my breasts,
caressing my belly,
whispering
to my thighs.

Sherrie Myers

Tempus Fugit (Carpe Diem)

Tempus fugit
tempus fuck it

That fish flew
a long time ago

Time
got away
in a haze of days
spent paying bills

and dues

Time wasted
always waiting
until that magic number
on the scales
somehow arrived

Now
tomorrow looms
more threat
than destination

Time
to seize that fish
and see what dish
you can make of it

before it gets away

THE DAYS OF FAT LILITH

FRANNIE ZELLMAN

First wife of Adam, according to Jewish-Talmudic legend, but before and after, a flying spirit goddess or demon, a spirit of the wind: *lilitu* (Sumerian), wind spirit. Spirit Daughter of Inanna, Spirit Mother of Astarte.

Lilith is fat and thin and fat again, flies free, happy in all shapes.

I

The Days of Fat Lilith

The Days of Fat Lilith

So frightened they were
of women—or spirits—
with the power to fly
or at least summon the wind
that they called me fat.
Notice that when they meet
woman-spirit with pride,
cleverness or ease,
it becomes fat.
Their own fright grows you.
Then it grows in you
that fat shapes of mind
body heart soul spirit
beyond
must be good
because the frightened
grew you
and their fright
flies with you
and makes you strong.

This was yet in the days
when my mother, Inanna,
stayed with me
and told me the names
of the things women spirits
prized: fire, earth, water, air,
especially air for me,
sky for her.
Yet she walked-danced

down to the bottom of Earth
to save her twin brother—
she, a sky dancer.

When she was about to leave,
she said, "They will only
try to shrink you
because they fear.
They try to shrink
all they fear
and rob it of wonder.
Fly off. Fly to wind
in a strange country.
They will not seek you."

When I tried to ask her
why I had to couple
with this human thing,
She called, already aloft,
"It is what is next,"
and waved.

How finite it was.
Its ignorance shone
through its fragile skin,
porous as godlings
but not as strong.
I laughed at its hanging
plexus.
Then it hated me.
We tried, but it was no good.

The thing accused me
of various crimes,
among them,
living with beasts
and other man-things.
I laughed again.

When the Universe
sent it another mate,
I cleared off.
Through the years
I watched as she
tried to please,
but the man-thing
imagined all kinds
of hate,
and accused her
of poisoning his mind.
Good and Evil, he said,
and drew his hate large
into an anger-God.

Serve him right
if I come to him
large as my new life
and free her,
I thought.
But I held off.
It was not my time.

I flew and gave winds
to other places,
other worlds,

other phases of being,
and flew with planet spirits.
I loved one especially
who turned day to night,
and had women spirits
gushing, in both senses.
All their senses.
Since he wasn't an earth spirit,
I cannot name him
for earth.
He still plays in me.

When time turned,
I came back.
Imagine what they now said:
baby snatcher, dream-killer,
man-gobbler.
Just for fun, I turned human
sometimes and watched
as they ran, calling
me new names they had
for my space:
fat, glob, blob, mountain,
cow, ugly, bitch, killer.
Somehow the great winds
took shape in their mind
as fear, once again,
and they feared women
of size.
Majesty.

You'd think
that if they feared/hated me,

they'd love the ones
who stayed small.
But far from it.
They ordered them, bullied them,
pressed them
to rub that plexis—
not from or with love,
but to escape it.

What a life.
A not-life.

Sometimes I took
unto myself
a woman
and taught her
the wind songs,
the power of air
and words.
And she brought others
and we danced
and flew through time
and day
and the cold season.
But she would die
and the songs died
soon after.

And all around flew up
words in so many languages,
words for the fear
that the man-things felt,
the fear of their own lack

turned to hate again:
Fat, night hag, evil.

One night,
as I flew in
with autumn
fire and harvest,
I realized that
fruits and animals
sowed and brought
forth
in the rhythm
of seasons
that the human-things
had lost,
and I found two or three
who understood.
I gave them back words
for growth
and softness
and becoming.

Then the curse.
"But we cannot
say that word,"
two wise ones said.
"It is linked with horror."
"The horror is fear,"
I told them,
"of what grows
and births
and changes."
Bodies all.

Bodies in spirits
and spirits in bodies.
It is the lack of separation
they call horror,
and frown
when it flies free
and moves
bright and thick.
"Fat," I said.
They swooned.

When they came to,
I grew myself to mountains
and they swooned again.

When they revived,
I told them the secret.

Suddenly they saw mountains
everywhere
charging, flying,
hanging in clouds.

A few still frightened
called the mountains "fat,"
and tried to run.
"Mountains are spirit, too,"
I told them. "My spirit.
Your mind.
The word: to grow,
to float high.
Is 'above' now forbidden?"

"Fat!" a few yelled,
and ran.
I lifted them easily
and thought
about sitting on them.
Instead I tossed them
into the coolness
of mountain air
and watched them land,
more frightened than before.

It was fun.
They were alone.
They had no words
because they'd refused mine.

All they could do
was stagger about,
silent, unthought.

The rest, however,
started to dance.
They grew.
They fatted.
They climbed mountains
in thought
and danced down,
as Inanna my mother
had danced to the under-earth.
But they learned to fly, too,
as she had taught me,
as I taught them.
Flight in word

growth in song
fear of birth and change
undone.

“Fat,” I said.
And they cheered.

We have now verbed “fat”
and untied it
from hate and fear.
Let it grow and fly
and birth.

For I am fat Lilith
come to grow peace
and these
are my born days.

Fat Lilith Plays

A fat wind spirit,
vast-armed,
can juggle air,
water, fire,
earth, time,
being, mind,
and body
so fast
that they blur
and cannot be separated
by all the eyes
in the Universe
that were, are,
or will ever be.

Flying Free

As a wind spirit,
I fly free
and I fly fat,
expanding as I fly,
taking in every country
invented or carved out
as I invent
or carve myself out
every time I fly
because as a fat wind spirit
I fill out my arms
my legs
my bottom
my stomach
whether I birth or not
and the spirits I birth
are fat, too.
They inherit
their mother's ether
and when they leave
earth and heave themselves
up up up
they leave, not their bodies,
but the worries
and fears
of earth people
who never did learn
how to do bodies
but keep trying to trim them,
bleach them

cut them:
psycho priestators
long ago
cursed flesh.

When we all fly together
bodies and spirits flash
in and out
and you'd swear
you don't know
which is which
or witch.

Love our fat wings.
They all
rise with you.

A Tree For Inanna

My mother, Inanna,
loved trees.
She loved the way
they gave over
to growing
so she could count rings
and know how old they were.

She loved flying
over the largest, fattest
olive trees,
as did her Greek and Turkish
and Asian friends
long before their countries
or names.

You can tell the worth
of a man-thing
by the way he loves or hates
trees
and honors the noblest oldest
fattest trees,
she said.

When my mother would
land on earth
she would sit
beneath the shade
of the oldest olive trees
and fan herself

with slings
made of their leaves
and tell me
what she had learned
on her last flight.

As I honor the girth
in myself
I honor her knowledge
and I love
the quiet of fat trees
who should be angry
with the man-things
who uproot them,
but instead
take root elsewhere
and teach, by their presence,
that what grows deepest
cannot be destroyed.

The Day I Left

The Man-Thing
called Adam
lay with me
and liked it
and liked me
until I told him
that I would
under no circumstances
walk behind.
Then he called me
an early word
meaning "fat"
as if to wound me
and I told him,
"Get another then.
I'm damned if I'll wear
those leaves.
I'm not scared
of my belly
and I like to dance.
Don't blame the snake.
He's already eyeing
your new wife."
I even asked him to dance one more time.
But he wouldn't.

I almost felt sorry
for him,
but as I flew my happy thick self
and thighs away

I remembered
that he wouldn't
let me teach him to fly.

When I Turn Human

I love the way
my breasts bounce
the way my behind bounces
the way my stomach tipples
and my hips float
as I learn again
to human walk

Spirit's fun and
flying is a hoot—
shout out to my owl friends—
but in human wise
I relearn flesh
and slipping my hands
all in and over,
wonder how humans
could possibly dislike
fat

Earth

I will stay here
on or above earth.
Night may come time
for flying,
but for day,
I will turn human
as I have for years
and fat my soul
on the good green things
and help humans
to keep them.

In The Rain

When the water
poured from
the skies,
Adam was frightened.
I comforted him
with my fat pretty
belly
and told him
that the garden
and the animals
all needed rain
to drink.
He said, "Should we
drink of it, too?"
I said, "Put your tongue
out and see."
It was rather funny
to see him stretching
his tongue
like a salamander
and tipping in the drops
as if they were nectar.
He said, "It is easier
to drink from
the falls nearby."
I said, "Well, now
you've tried rainwater.
Maybe one day
you can eat snow."
"What is snow?"

he asked.
"Like rain,
but prettier and colder,"
I said.
I could see him
trying to work
his brain around "colder,"
although "prettier"
seemed easy enough.
"It won't happen here,"
I explained.
"This climate is too warm."
Climate—he considered this.
"There are other places, then,"
he said.
"Many," I agreed.
"But we must stay here."
"That is your fear talking,"
I said.
"Why doesn't yours talk?"
he muttered.
"Because I've been
to many other places,"
I said.
"Fear doesn't run in them."

He was not happy
about that.
I danced in the rain,
my thick breasts
dappled with water.

His opinion of rain
changed over
as quickly
as a snake sheds
its skin.

Joke, Adam.
Just a joke.
Let me dry you
with these leaves.

Of Sky, Wind and Love

The Great Sky Dancer,
Inanna, bore me,
Fat Lilith.
I in turn
have now borne
Astarte.
My mother
danced through space
and clouds,
delighting the gods.
I, wind-spirit,
flew above earth
and around it,
bringing the good air
and rain.
Astarte, my daughter,
will sing lust
and pirouette
her own brand of love.
Men will confuse it
with longing.

Women, however,
will reap
what I have sown
and will feel
through their hair
the wind and rain

like lovers.

They blossom
in their own fields
and time.

Time

1
The Thin Time

I laughed to see
men trying to divide
day and night
summer and winter
into smaller slabs
of knowledge
so that they could
force others to toil
for them
and justify
the theft.

2

I liked seasons,
but months seemed
itchy and bothersome.

3

Newer Fatter Time?

Yet now they cast
for bigger and bigger slabs—
ages, eras, epochs, periods, eons.

These are names

for expanding
past fear.

Perhaps one day soon
they may come around
to fatting time again
after all.

Mystery

Men of many religions
have tried to own
or disown me,
insisting
that I am thin or fat
or two-bodied
or four-headed
or ghostly,
that I do or do not
rob their strength,
consort with demons,
ruin crops,
deceive merchants.
Yet what I bring
and honor—
as Fat Lilith
human and spirit—
is simply
the wind.

Is this so frightening?

Astarte

I raised you,
my soft happy-curved beloved,
to bring love.

Remember that
when men
try to abstract
your warmth
and box it

into body parts
swinging
from a photo.

II

The Birthing

The Birthing

Through time
but not time.
Inanna, my mother,
said, "We have always been,
but then a breath conceives us,
yet we ourselves conceive
at that time.
You have always been,
but I thought you
into being
and stars swirled,
and fires danced,
and water flowed.
You sang your way
out of me,
not in words
but in sounds.
You were a happy child."

You loved to play
on other planets,
and you would tell me.
We know of the beings
from the World of Water
and the Fire Planet.
He had green hair.
Eyes like coal.
"In love?" I asked.
You smiled.

“I didn’t want
to leave you,”
my mother said.

But she did.

Body

Somewhere along the line
there are borders.
First, you are space
and thoughts.
Then you grow
into mind.
Pointing out
like a theorem,
you meet lines
but push beyond,
each line tripping
new lines.
Veins, heart, arms,
legs, shoulders.
In one space
like a human,
In another,
more.
You expand,
more again
than a body,
as if thought
propelled you
into larger than
body, and your mind
flew the galaxy
and back.

Then you stop,
finite.
At least for now.

Size

Humans fear
infinity
more than
anything
or anyone.
And yet
no one teaches us
to be finite.
Trees, grass,
small animals:
They fill
their own spaces,
functions,
birth and die
only to birth again.
We, on the other hand,
sweep through air,
water, become
fire, then stone.
This is how humans
worship: stone of
temple, gate, furze,
votary.
This is how they cut
us to size,
make us accessible.

Flying

They teach you early
to point up,
to rush the air,
to blaze
through nights.
Humans will see you
but don't worry,
they say.
They will think
you are not
or are, at most,
a trick
of their minds.

Don't worry.
Sky and new sun
warm,
nights cool.

Meanwhile,
friend your air.

Night

The first humans
huddled in caves
and asked to live.
I pitied them
and made fire
to heat them.
But thousands of years
later, they spoke
of Prometheus.
They named
lights and gave them
stars.
"Look," I told them,
"dark is only
a different light,
not absence.
Think sleek air
fine as snow
that travels
in tides.
Water on the moon,
a spanning out
across sleep."

I taught them
the hours
when sleep
quickens, brings
portents, strange
news.

When they
lived through the fright,
they named dreams.

I flew, fat and eased,
through their time.

Rain

I asked the humans,
"Who gave you rain?"
They couldn't answer,
although they knew
fire quickly enough.
Air? No.
Earth? Not.
But rain? Have they seen
the sparks that fly
when rain glances
off what they call
my body?
Fire water, earthen air.
Green wire, slant of purple
to match the hour
before sleep,
late after sunrise.
Night is my time.
On their earth
mist falls into gutters,
brings rainbows.
City talk.
Night rain.

If they are lucky,
I will rub the drops
from my thick body
to bless their dawn.

Seasons

For humans,
time passes
to months:
cold, flakes, drops,
sun to fields.
Thunder pricks lightning.
Then back to heat,
cold again,
their houses grown
now to comfort
but still creaking
in wind.

One day
I will teach them
to summon
warmth.

Love

Once upon a time
humans coupled.
Sometimes new humans
arrived.
Entirely satisfying
until poets
in France
hinted at more.

Where I roam
there are shades
of want
in many.
They occupy
each other,
then go,
find each other,
then fly off again.

I only knew more
when I taught humans,
when I had my daughter,
when the humans hurt.

Coupling

We join
all, not just parts.
Thought summons thought
and weaves through,
pressing against.
Humans, especially,
think only bodies.

If you look
in the mists,
where we gather,
you may see
our grey, unchecked
light.

Shapes

"Humans think
their bodies
into one shape,"
my mother said.
"But we shine
fluid."

Fat and Thin

"You can choose,"
Inanna said.
"Sometimes fat,
with strong, full arms
and a glowing belly.
Sometimes thin
with legs like vines,
face at right angles.
Sometimes both.
Humans confuse
shape with intent.
Sometimes they fear growth.
Rain evens out
their flint.
Then they sleep."

Sleep

"Humans fade
when they sleep,"
my mother said.
"How do you know?"
I asked.
"I've seen a few."
She winked.
Great winker, my mother.
Her eye dove under,
but glowed.
How did she do it?
"They didn't know,
did they?"
"No. To them,
I was a dream."
"Were they happy
on waking?"
"Incredibly."

Poising myself
just on the edge
of believability,
I watched myself
into their sleep.
"To me," I told them
as their mouths opened
and flapped closed,
"you are the dream."

Full Moon One

When I was young,
Inanna used to
give me moon baths.
She would take me
outside
and lift my arms
into the torrent
of silver
pouring.
Then she would strip
and do the same.
I never forgot
her arms raised,
skin brighter
than any moon,
her mouth open
in chant,
exulting,
singing
as our forebears
sang,
but in joy.
"Cast us up,"
she called.
"We flow
in you.
Bring us
like wine
to seas
whose shores

we know
only from
what they sang,
the old ones
on their hills
before we came
and split their nights."
There was more
about making clear
at the full.

When she stopped,
the forest
seemed to stop, too:
Noises I hadn't known
I knew
deserted.
I would have spoken,
but she held up a hand.
Soon the noises rolled again,
and the creatures
snuffled or chirped or mewed.

"How did you do that?"
I asked in awe.
"The silence."

She smiled.
Irritating, magical,
alluring, her words
like herself, always:
"One day,
you will know."

Dreams

For humans,
dreams arrive
in night-dark,
although they also
confuse them
with wishes.
Imagine: Days pass,
dreamless, static,
everything disparate,
alone.
For me: Inanna.
She counsels,
argues, comforts,
reveals. “Don’t laugh,”
she says, “but humans
think you join
their bodies.”
I laughed. “I’ve
better things to do
in dreams.”

Belly

Sometimes
I have a belly
when I want
to hug the little things
to me.
Comfort, the human word.

Children

They accuse me
of kidnapping.
Untrue. Children like
to play,
and so do I.
Teach them the howl
of wind,
the songs of birds,
the hiss of small streams,
the growl of thunder,
the silence of clouds,
and they follow,
wanting to feed
their senses,
never sated.

Anger

When one of
the humans
puts his hand
on a child
to hurt,
my eyes go
the red
they term hellish
and my own fist
crumples the human
into twiggish bones.

At least that's
what they say.

Cities

So many kinds
of light.
I didn't like them
at first,
All the humans
running at each other,
metal bugs snorting
as they carried humans,
steel saws prowling
as they made streets.
Vertical honeycombs
they could see out,
but others couldn't.

This is later.
The first cities
rose from sand.
I liked their mornings:
quiet, cool,
washed like desert
flowers springing up
after the forty years'
rain.

These days
I march through
their crowds,
strangely invisible.

Birthing–2

I thought her
into being,
but she sat
in my body
like a human.

When it was time,
she laughed her way
out.

The Moon–2

I taught them
to dance
in silver light.

Toward morning,
they lay down
on the grass
as if drunk.

But I knew
it was only
sky-sickness,
wishing, receiving,
overcome
with blessings
too bright.

Mother

"As I do
with you,
so will you do,"
Inanna said
as she held, bathed,
fed, burped, hugged,
slapped, cradled me.

Strange as it sounds,
Astarte didn't want
to be held much.
She ventured away
from my body,
ran to the streams,
kissed flowers.
But she liked meadows,
not wild growth.
I hailed her lushness,
hoping she would
pull toward it.
"Our fat juicy souls
are for wanting
and play," I said.
"I know," she said,
and praised her lovers.

Flowers

I held the heart
of a rose
to her cheek.
Astarte sniffed.
She smiled,
then removed
her top garment,
revealing
large round tan breasts
that swung back
and forth
as she worked
her blossomed hips
and stomach folds.
"Very nice,"
I said.
"But all from
a rose?"
"I was thinking
of my nipples
as the hearts
of smaller flowers,"
she said.
I stayed behind a tree.
A woman and a man
approached.
They bowed and knelt.
"Will you dance?" I whispered.
She laughed.
"Let them dance,"

she said.
“I am their lust.”
“Love?” I asked.
“No matter what
priests say,
They’re not separate.”
“Perhaps one day,”
she said.
“All I know now
is that touch
runs through me.
And through them.
We are happy.”

Snow

If snow had fallen
in the place I was born,
the ground would
have held cold
for at least
half a season.
The stones and grass
told a different story.
Inanna spoke of snow
when I was still
at her knee.
She delighted
in the shapes of ice
and the way
it turned to pearl
and sticks.
"One day," she said,
"you will see it."

When I climbed,
then became mountain,
there were parts
that turned frozen.
Things that shone
in the dark,
then melted,
flowed back to water,
then to freezing.
When the moon hit
my still warm flow,

we turned silver.

“This is like
bathing in the moon,
but better,” I told Inanna,
who no longer visited.
Yet I could swear
I heard her say,
somehow, somewhere,
“Cold is the way
we rest.”

Happy

I have learned
that moments
of human life
cause them
to feel
as if they
have made
connections
with those
they label
gods.

Pain

To see
the few
I cherished
die.

Father

When I asked Inanna,
she said,
"Many. None."
"Some people say
from the sky?"
"Maybe. But not only."
"How can that be?"
"We breed differently.
All the males I loved
formed part of you,
as they loved me."
"Will I know them?"
"As they show themselves
in you."

I did not tell her
that I imagined
just one.

It was rainy, anyway,
and all love
stayed indoors
that day.
No reflections.

If he existed,
I thought,
he would surely
tenant a brighter
world.

Gods

They call us
this.
Then they call
upon us.
It is our burden,
to try
to help them
when we know
that we are
travelers, as they are,
perhaps with more
powers, calling up
certainties of nature
rather than sky magic.

We tell them
not to worship,
but to greet
and join.

III

The Loves of Fat Lilith

Slow Rain

All kinds of weather,
but especially
the slow rain
that drips into
bright colored runs
near sidewalks
and slides warm
across my skin
summering
like rich humans
in places
they rub
with oil.

I drink
you
into all my
creases.
Folds shimmer.

Fat Lilith,
too wild and rich
for dry plains.

Vanbor

The way humans
pronounce it.
On other planets
there are also cynics.
He didn't believe much,
didn't care to.
He played to my skeptic
good-naturedly,
as a sated cat
plays with
a frightened mouse
she might or might not
eat.
He knew how to move
so slowly
and assuredly
along my fat arms.
His fingers never did
an unplanned thing.
Even when they skimmed
lower, they flew,
then drifted in my juice,
then crashed deep.

He said I rode well
and loved the way
my stomach bounced
over his male set
(like humans,
but he had two).

Chocolate

We taught humans
to harvest it
long before it became
our food.
"Why this strange bean?"
they asked.
"One day," I said,
it will make your mouths
smile."

Music

We taught humans
to sing.
Then we showed them
instruments.
Some humans sing
almost like Vanbor.
The notes curl
from their windpipes
and they hunt them
deep into the earth
part of their chests.
So selfish of me,
to want the deep singers
who resemble
the deepest one.

Cats

It's about
the way their fur ripples
when they stand, sit or jump.
As god forces, we see energy
like fire glowing through them
that whirls, then sleeps.
When they stalk, spun silver.

Purring
to soothe anxieties;
loud purring
to vanquish.

Petting.

Mother of Mothers

"Who was she?"
I asked Inanna.
I couldn't get the name.
"Before these lands
turned to dust,
she loved their trees.
Olives, dates, lemons.
She tamed their birds.

"Before that, when
the earth shook
all around,
humans prayed.
They feared her."
"Did you?" I asked.
"Not her words," she said.
"But mostly when
she left and I
had to learn new magic."
"Will I ever see her?"
"Maybe in your dreams."

Vulva

Imagine dark feathers
over not a few inches,
but a field.
I shocked my lovers
by growing it.
They didn't know where
to look or turn.
One, though, wanted
to heat his face.
He rubbed the length
of it,
snuffling like a boar.
Then he put his mouth
to the thick curls over it.
"Rain and earth," he pronounced.
That made me so wet
that a river was born.

He had to climb
to outrun the flood.

Pomegranates

Seeds so red
that they shame
evening sun,
blood, fire.
Humans eat
only the spruce
flesh, but we crunch
the seeds,
loving the bitter
sluice against
our tongues.

Just sweet
would bore.

Seasons–2

Summer

Olives and lemons.
Tart and sour.
Hot as breath,
the sun in our mouths,
breathing on our skin.
But best, water
of the sea, dark and cool
on our warm, salty bodies.

Autumn

Leaf piles, tree skins.
Inanna taught me
to run in them, stamping
as I played.
As Fat Lilith, I loved
the shorter afternoons,
wide evenings,
cooling as they lengthened
out to stars.

And at night,
I would call the moon.

Winter

The sky makes
water which turns

breath into silver.

I fly sharp into
the terror of
bright cold.

Spring

Rivers give up
their ice so fast
that I flow into
them late
when gardens
are already soft
underfoot
and I flesh out
into fat as stippled
as new calves
and almost as wet.

Spring 2: Newborn Animals

Helpless, wet, eyes closed,
our fear and wonder.
When they open their eyes
and stand,
the world spins
at a different angle
and every voice for miles
around
hushes, then speaks caution
along with mothers
who stand both aghast

at their creations
and too awed
to be proud.

Astarte–2

"I don't need to fly,"
she said.
I felt as if she'd slapped me.
"Darling, whyever not?"
"I will fly without wings."
She made a circle
with her hands.
"In minds," I said.
"And bodies. That is
how I play.
When I feel a man
opening to me,
it's better than flying."
I understood.
But if you ask me,
I'd rather fly.
"In our ways,
we catch the head
of the storm," I said.
She laughed.
"I heed the rain.
You ride the wind."

And that is how
we left it.

The Ways of Fat Lilith

She shall be fat, thin,
bodied, bodiless,
warm, cold, angry,
calm, gentle,
sad, happy, wondering,
accepting, questioning.

She shall wander and fly,
then touch down on a wave
like some sea bird
or engine.

She shall make night
her own,
then wave her infinite hand
over the first of morning.

She shall see and touch
humans, blend,
then divide from them,
understand, then reject,
embrace, reclaim,
advise, reverse,
separate, unite,
tower above them,
huddle with them
around fires
near oceans,

above the wind.

She shall bring them
known, unknown roots,
the plants of bulbs,
ways to hunt,
speech of many lands,
but most of all,
the rules and wonder
of flying
for those ready
to know it.

Biographies

Kathy Barron

It's been quite a ride, this life.
I'm about to turn fifty-six and I'm looking back and
looking forward.
Part of my real healing has been taking time away
from relationships, living my life without
any thought of any man.
I needed this time and space—
I'm not sure if or when it will ever end,
only that I'm so much more whole and happy than
when I was
looking for love and validation outside of myself.

Since our first book came out
I lost my mom, who was my best friend, to cancer,
I divorced my narcissistic, pathologically lying
husband.
I've survived my own cancer and breaking both arms
at once.
I've been teaching high school English for two years.
I've been living in Florida the past eight years.
I'm about to move across the country to Colorado
to be near my daughter, still and always the heart
of my life.
A new adventure into a new life.
I'm bringing with me the lessons learned,
my reclaimed power, and my fire.
I'm interested to see where my new path leads.

Durette Hauser

Durette Hauser is a tax accountant who lives in Laingsburg, Michigan. She has owned her own accounting and tax business since 1989. She loves traveling, trying new foods and recipes, reading, swimming, yoga, bluegrass music, living life to the fullest, her body, and attending loving retreats.

Her first positive exposure to fat acceptance was reading the book *Wake Up, I'm Fat!* by Camryn Manheim. She first attended an Abundia retreat in 2004. She had never heard of Health at Every Size (HAES) until that retreat. The very idea that being fat was acceptable totally rocked her world. Since then she has taken a journey on the Spiral of Acceptance towards better health and happiness.

She hopes to see more women learn about the concept of Health at Every Size. The Abundia Retreat is the perfect place to come and be loved by many other fat women and to learn to love yourself more.

Tolonda Henderson

Tolonda Henderson is an MA/PhD student in English at the University of Connecticut specializing in children's literature. A Harry Potter scholar, Mx. Henderson has recently published an essay on the social construction of fatness in the series (see *Inside the World of Harry Potter* from MacFarland Press).

Their hobbies include crochet and tap dancing in their living room. Mx. Henderson's poems have also been published in *Melancholy Hyperbole, Yellow Chair Press,* and *Freeze Ray Poetry.*

Dawn Howard

Dawn Howard is in the process of reinventing her life. For thirty years her identity was based upon her role as a workaholic document controller in the male-dominated business of engineering. She lives in the southwest suburbs of Chicago with her dogs, a little pack of rescue chihuahuas and chihuahua mixes.

Everything changed when within nine years she lost her father, husband, and mother. Following the death of her father she cared for her mother, who had dementia/Alzheimer's, and also for her husband, who was left disabled following back surgery and eighteen months later died suddenly from a brain aneurysm.

Dawn has always been a writer, writing poetry, erotica, short stories, resumes, website content, or policies and procedures for her employers.

She is an advocate for body and fat acceptance, and has been since her twenties, when she discovered Cheri Erdman's book *Nothing to Lose.* Dawn eventually joined the board of Abundia, an annual retreat for women of size, until she resigned following the death of her husband. Cheri Erdman was one of the founders of Abundia.

In the past six years Dawn has learned to belly dance and was invited to join a troupe, Real Women Bellydance, that has members of all shapes, sizes, and ages. She dabbled in burlesque classes, explored nudism, and fell in love with yoga. She became vocal about sex positivity and a woman's right to pleasure, and her photo was included in Elle Chase's book *Curvy Girl Sex.* More recently she has been studying magick, witchcraft, and Wicca, and has become more involved in the Pagan community.

Miranda Jacobson

Miranda Jacobson is a freelance journalist, author, and now poet, thanks to the Fat Poets' Society. Her writing covers numerous topics, and she is published in newsletters and journals that cover various interests.

She has been battling poor self-image thought patterns inherited from her family her entire life. When she herself was a skinny preteen her family went on a very strict diet—an unnecessary and undesirable activity for an 11-yeat-old girl—and for anyone else!

She writes from her personal experiences and feelings.

Sherrie Myers

Sherrie Myers lives in the Mojave Desert in southern California with her husband, Gerald. She is owned by a number of cats, including Orange, who likes to offer his own input into her writing and make the occasional comment to her friends in chat.

Lesleigh Owen

In my forty-five years on this planet, I have accomplished many things for which I feel a blush of pride. I mean, how many people can juggle a ridiculously happy marriage, a rock-and-roll activism schedule, and a commitment to attaining true Crazy Cat Lady status? However, one of my proudest accomplishments remains publishing my fat pride poetry in all three volumes of *Fat*

Poets Speak.

Since the publication of the first *Fat Poets Speak* in 2009, a bunch has changed. With the introduction of fat and confident characters like Carmen Wade, Plum Kettle, and Titus Andromedon, pop culture has dipped its big toe in the waters of fat positivity. I am heartened.

But. Yesterday, while ordering fried pickles (because yum!), my server food-shamed me. Two days ago, one of my students linked fatness, poverty, fast food consumption, and illness—all in a single sentence. This, after I'd regaled the class with anecdotes about interviewing fat folks for my dissertation, which focused on—you guessed it—stigma against fat people.

So, yeah, I am heartened by the cultural progress we're making, inch by painful inch, but I also recognize we have a long, long, long way to go.

Fat Poets Speak 3: FatDance Flying contributes to this culture of change. We share our stories of stigma, pride, pain, and hope, all rendered through lenses of fatness. The third installment in the *Fat Poets Speak* series continues to center the experiences of fat folks and make legible the grammar of our lives.

I am so proud to once again be a part of this lofty and beautiful project.

Michelle Kriz Parkinson

I wish I could remember the first time anyone told me it was okay to be fat—or that I had believed that person then. I do know it's something I had to hear a number of times to even consider, and that's why it's something I say over and over again now for whoever might need to hear it.

As a younger poet, I often shied away from the vulnerable, causing a professor to advise me to write greeting cards instead of poems. Though he meant it as an insult, that's actually where my career path led, and now I make a living creating the tools for people to connect with one another.

I'm constantly in awe of the power of words, and though I identify as both fat and a poet, I'd never embraced fatness as a topic for my poetry until I discovered the Fat Poets' Society. It was so freeing to allow the truth I hold in my body to flow onto the page.

In addition to general fattery, I love to travel, pet dogs, go to the theatre, swim, cook, fight for social justice, challenge expectations, and embrace clichés. I live in Cleveland, Ohio with one husband, two dogs, and over 300 bottles of nail polish.

Kris Owen

has elected not to submit a biography.

Frannie Zellman

With every year we seem to get closer to fat acceptance, as more people become involved in the Fat Acceptance movement and the field of Fat Studies acquires more material, more scholars, and more professors.

What we still need is a Fat Poetry Conference, with poets from around the world who write about what it means to be fat and happy and sad and excited and angry and proud. In other words, what it means to be and live as a fat person.

One day, we will have one.

Meanwhile, dance and fly with us as we rise.

About Pearlsong Press

Pearlsong Press is an independent publishing company dedicated to providing books and resources that entertain while expanding perspectives on the self and the world. The company was founded by psychologist Peggy Elam, Ph.D.

Fiction

If We Were Snowflakes—YA novel by Barbara D'Souza
Heretics: A Love Story & *The Singing of Swans*—
novels about the divine feminine by Mary Saracino
Judith—an historical novel by Leslie Moïse
Fatropolis—paranormal adventure by Tracey L. Thompson
The Falstaff Vampire Files, Bride of the Living Dead, Larger Than Death, Large Target, At Large & *A Ton of Trouble*—
paranormal adventure, romantic comedy & mysteries by Lynne Murray
The Season of Lost Children—a novel by Karen Blomain
Fallen Embers & *Blowing Embers*—Books 1 & 2 of The Embers Series, paranormal romance by Lauri J Owen
The Program & *The Fat Lady Sings*—suspense & YA novels by Charlie Lovett
Syd Arthur—a novel by Ellen Frankel
Measure By Measure—a romantic romp with the fabulously fat by Rebecca Fox & William Sherman
FatLand & *FatLand: The Early Days*—Books 1 & 2 of The FatLand Trilogy by Frannie Zellman

Romance Novels & Short Stories Featuring Big Beautiful Heroines

by Pat Ballard, the Queen of Rubenesque Romances:
Once Upon Another Time | *Adam & Evelyn* | *ASAP Nanny* | *Dangerous Love* | *The Best Man* | *Abigail's Revenge* | *Dangerous Curves Ahead: Short Stories* | *Wanted: One Groom* | *Nobody's Perfect* | *His Brother's Child* | *A Worthy Heir*
by Rebecca Brock—*The Giving Season*

& by Judy Bagshaw—*Kiss Me, Nate!* & *At Long Last, Love*

Nonfiction

Flying On Invisible Wings—poetry by Félix Garmendía
Other Nations: An Animal Journal—poetry by Maria Famà
Soul Mothers' Wisdom: Seven Insights for the Single Mother by Bette J. Freedson
Acceptable Prejudice? Fat, Rhetoric & Social Justice & *Talking Fat: Health vs. Persuasion in the War on Our Bodies* by Lonie McMichael, Ph.D.
Hiking the Pack Line: Moving from Grief to a Joyful Life by Bonnie Shapbell
A Life Interrupted: Living with Brain Injury—poetry by Louise Mathewson
ExtraOrdinary: An End of Life Story Without End—memoir by Michele Tamaren & Michael Wittner
Love is the Thread: A Knitting Friendship by Leslie Moïse, Ph.D.
Fat Poets Speak: Voices of the Fat Poets' Society & *Fat Poets Speak 2: Living and Loving Fatly*—Frannie Zellman, Ed.
10 Steps to Loving Your Body (No Matter What Size You Are) & *Something to Think About: Reflections on Life, Family, Body Image & Other Weighty Matters by the Queen of Rubenesque Romances* by Pat Ballard
Beyond Measure: A Memoir About Short Stature & Inner Growth by Ellen Frankel
Taking Up Space: How Eating Well & Exercising Regularly Changed My Life by Pattie Thomas, Ph.D. with Carl Wilkerson, M.B.A.
Off Kilter: A Woman's Journey to Peace with Scoliosis, Her Mother & Her Polish Heritage—memoir by Linda C. Wisniewski
Unconventional Means: The Dream Down Under—spiritual travelogue by Anne Richardson Williams
Splendid Seniors: Great Lives, Great Deeds—inspirational biographies by Jack Adler

www.ingramcontent.com/pod-product-compliance
Ingram Content Group UK Ltd.
Pitfield, Milton Keynes, MK11 3LW, UK
UKHW041955190726
13854UKWH00005B/1995

9 781597 190954